John Newton

Thoughts Upon the African Slave Trade

John Newton

Thoughts Upon the African Slave Trade

ISBN/EAN: 9783744793704

Printed in Europe, USA, Canada, Australia, Japan

Cover: Foto ©ninafisch / pixelio.de

More available books at **www.hansebooks.com**

AFRICAN SLAVE TRADE.

By JOHN NEWTON,

RECTOR OF ST. MARY WOOLNOTH.

MATT. vii. 12.

ALL THINGS WHATSOEVER YE WOULD THAT MEN SHOULD DO TO YOU,
DO YE EVEN SO TO THEM: FOR THIS IS THE LAW AND THE PRO-
PHETS.

HOMO SUM ——

LONDON:

PRINTED FOR J. BUCKLAND, IN PATER-NOSTER-ROW; AND
J. JOHNSON, IN ST. PAUL'S CHURCH-YARD.
M.DCC.LXXXVIII.

THOUGHTS

UPON THE

AFRICAN SLAVE TRADE.

THE nature and effects of that unhappy and difgraceful branch of commerce, which has long been maintained on the Coaft of Africa, with the fole, and profeffed defign of purchafing our fellow-creatures, in order to fupply our Weft-India iflands and the American colonies, when they were ours, with Slaves; is now generally underftood. So much light has been thrown upon the fubject, by many able pens; and fo many refpectable perfons have already engaged to ufe their utmoft influence, for the fuppreffion of a traffic, which contradicts the feelings of humanity; that it is hoped, this ftain of our National character will foon be wiped out.

B   If

If I attempt, after what has been done, to throw my mite into the public ſtock of information, it is leſs from an apprehenſion that my interference is neceſſary, than from a conviction, that ſilence, at ſuch a time, and on ſuch an occaſion, would, in me, be criminal. If my teſtimony ſhould not be neceſſary, or ſerviceable, yet, perhaps, I am bound, in conſcience, to take ſhame to myſelf by a public confeſſion, which, however ſincere, comes too late to prevent, or repair, the miſery and miſchief to which I have, formerly, been acceſſary.

I hope it will always be a ſubject of humiliating reflection to me, that I was, once, an active inſtrument, in a buſineſs at which my heart now ſhudders. My headſtrong paſſions and follies plunged me, in early life, into a ſucceſſion of difficulties and hardſhips, which, at length, reduced me to ſeek a refuge among the Natives of Africa There, for about the ſpace of eighteen months, I was in effect, though without the name, a Captive and a Slave myſelf ; and was depreſſed to the loweſt degree of human wretchedneſs. Poſſibly, I ſhould not have been ſo completely miſerable, had I lived among the Natives only, but it was my lot to reſide with white men ; for at that time, ſeveral perſons of my own colour

and

and language were fettled upon that part of the Windward coaft, which lies between Sierra-Leon and Cape Mount; for the purpofe of purchafing and collecting Slaves, to fell to the veffels that arrived from Europe.

This is a bourn, from which few travellers return, who have once determined to venture upon a temporary refidence there; but the good providence of God, without my expectation, and almoft againft my will, delivered me from thofe fcenes of wickednefs and woe; and I arrived at Liverpool in May 1748. I foon revifited the place of my captivity, as mate of a fhip, and, in the year 1750, I was appointed commander, in which capacity I made three voyages to the Windward Coaft, for Slaves.

I firft faw the Coaft of Guinea in the year 1745, and took my laft leave of it in 1754. It was not, intentionally, a farewel; but through the mercy of God it proved fo. I fitted out for a fourth voyage, and was upon the point of failing, when I was arrefted by a fudden illnefs, and I refigned the fhip to another Captain.

Thus I was unexpectedly freed from this difagreeable fervice. Difagreeable I had long

found

found it; but I think I fhould have quitted it
fooner, had I confidered it, as I now do, to be
unlawful and wrong.   But I never had a fcru-
ple upon this head at the time; nor was fuch
a thought once fuggefted to me, by any friend.
What I did, I did ignorantly; confidering it
as the line of life which Divine Providence
had allotted me, and having no concern, in
point of confcience, but to treat the Slaves,
while under my care, with as much humanity
as a regard to my own fafety would admit.

The experience and obfervation of nine
years, would qualify me for being a compe-
tent witnefs upon this fubject, could I fafely
truft to the report of Memory, after an interval
of more than thirty-three years.   But, in the
courfe of fo long a period, the ideas of paft
fcenes and tranfactions, grow indiftinct; and I
am aware, that what I have feen, and what I
have only heard related, may, by this time,
have become fo infenfibly blended together,
that, in fome cafes, it may be difficult for me,
if not impoffible, to diftinguifh them, with
abfolute certainty.   It is, however, my earneft
defire, and will therefore engage my utmoft
care, that I may offer nothing in writing, as
from my own knowledge, which I could not
chearfully, if requifite, confirm upon oath.

That

That part of the African fhore, which lies between the river Sierra-Leon, lat. 8. 30. N. and Cape Palmas, is ufually known by the name of the Windward, or Grain Coaft. The extent (if my recollection does not fail me) is about one hundred and fifty leagues. There is a fort upon Benee Ifland, in Sierra-Leon, which formerly belonged to the old African Company: they alfo had a fort on an ifland in the river Sherbro; but the former was in private hands, and of the latter, fcarcely the foundations were vifible, when I firft went to Africa. There is no fort, or factory, upon this coaft, under the fanction of our Government; but there were, as I have faid, and probably ftill are, private traders refident at Benec Ifland, at the Bananoes, and at the Plantanes. The former of thefe is about twelve, and the latter twenty leagues, from Sierra-Leon, to the South-Eaft.

By thefe perfons, the trade is carried on, in boats and fhallops, thirty or forty leagues to the northward, in feveral rivers lying within the fhoals of Rio Grande. But the moft northerly place of trade, for fhipping, is Sierra-Leon, and the bufinefs there, and in that neighbourhood, is chiefly tranfacted with the white men: but from Sherbro to Cape Palmas, directly with

the

the natives. Though I have been on the Gold
Coaft, and beyond it as far as Cape Lopez, in
the latitude of one or two degrees South, I pro-
fefs no knowledge of the African trade, but
as it was conducted on the Windward Coaft,
when I was concerned in it.

I am not qualified, and if I were, I fhould
think it rather unfuitable to my prefent character, as a Minifter of the Gofpel, to confider
the African Slave Trade, merely, in a political
light. This difquifition more properly be-
longs to perfons in civil life. Only thus far
my character as a Minifter will allow, and perhaps require me, to obferve, that the beft Human Policy, is that which is connected with a
reverential regard to Almighty God, the Su-
preme Governor of the Earth. Every plan, which
aims at the welfare of a nation, in defiance of
his authority and laws, however apparently
wife, will prove to he effentially defective,
and, if perfifted in, ruinous. The Righteous
Lord loveth Righteoufnefs, and He has engaged to plead the caufe, and vindicate the
wrongs of the oppreffed. It is Righteoufnefs
that exalteth a nation ; and Wickednefs is the
prefent reproach, and will, fooner or later,
unlefs repentance intervene, prove the ruin of
any people.

Perhaps

Perhaps what I have faid of myfelf may be applicable to the nation at large. The Slave Trade was always unjuftifiable; but in-attention and intereft prevented, for a time, the evil from being perceived. It is otherwife at prefent; the mifchiefs and evils, connected with it, have been, of late years, reprefented with fuch undeniable evidence, and are now fo generally known, that I fuppofe there is hardly an objection can be made, to the wifh of thoufands, perhaps of millions, for the fup-preffion of this Trade, but upon the ground of political expedience.

Tho' I were even fure, that a principal branch of the public revenue depended upon the African Trade (which, I apprehend, is far from being the cafe), if I had accefs and influence, I fhould think myfelf bound to fay to Government, to Parliament, and to the Nation, " It is not law-" ful to put it into the Treafury, becaufe it is " the price of blood *."

I account an intelligent Farmer to be a good Politician, in this fenfe; that, if he has a large heap of good corn, he will not put a fmall quantity, that is damaged, to the reft, for the fake of encreafing the heap. He knows

* Matth. xxvii. 6.

that

that fuch an addition would fpoil the whole. God forbid, that any fuppofed profit or advantage, which we can derive from the groans and agonie, and blood of the poor Africans, fhould draw down his heavy curfe, upon all that we might, otherwife, honourably and comfortably poffefs.

For the fake of Method, I could wifh to confider the African Trade,—Firft, with regard to the effects it has upon our own people; and Secondly, as it concerns the Blacks, or, as they *are* more contemptuoufly ftyled, the Negroe Slaves, whom we purchafe upon the Coaft. But thefe two topics are fo interwoven together, that it will not be eafy to keep them exactly feparate.

1. The firft point I fhall mention is furely of political importance, if the lives of our fellow-fubjects be fo; and if a rapid lofs of Seamen deferves the attention of a maritime people. This lofs, in the African Trade, is truly alarming. I admit, that many of them are cut off in their firft voyage, and, confequently, before they can properly rank as Seamen; though they would have been Seamen, if they had lived. But the neighbourhood of our fea-ports is continually drained, of men and boys, to fupply the places of thofe who

die

die abroad; and if they are not all Seamen, they are all our brethren and countrymen, fubjects of the Britifh Government.

The people who remain, on fhip-board, upon the open coaft, if not accuftomed to the climate, are liable to the attack of an inflammatory fever, which is not often fatal, unlefs the concurrence of unfavourable circumftances makes it fo. When this danger is over, I think they might, probably, be as healthy as in moft other voyages ; provided, they could be kept from fleeping in the dews, from being much expofed to the rain, from the intemperate ufe of fpirits, and efpecially from women.

But, confidering the general difpofition of our Sailors, and the nature of the Slave Trade, thefe provifos are of little more fignificance, than if I fhould fay, upon another occafion, that Great-Britain would be a happy country, *provided*, all the inhabitants were Wife, and Good. The Sailors *muft be* much expofed to the weather; efpecially on the Windward Coaft, where a great part of the cargo is procured by boats, which are often fent to the diftance of thirty or forty leagues, and are fometimes a month before they return. Many veffels arrive upon the coaft before the rainy

C   feafon,

feafon, which continues from about May to October, is over; and if trade be fcarce, the fhips which arrive in the fair, or dry feafon, often remain till the rains return, before they can complete their purchafe. A proper fhelter from the weather, in an open boat, when the rain is inceffant night and day, for weeks and months, is impracticable.

I have myfelf, in fuch a boat, been five or fix days together, without, as we fay, a dry thread about me, fleeping or waking. And during the fair feafon, Tornadoes, or violent ftorms of wind, thunder, and heavy rain, are very frequent, though they feldom laft long. In fact, the boats feldom return, without bringing fome of the people ill of dangerous fevers or fluxes, occafioned either by the weather, or by unwholfome diet, fuch as the crude fruits and palm wine, with which they are plentifully fupplied by the natives.

Strong liquors, fuch as brandy, rum, or Englifh fpirits, the Sailors cannot often procure, in fuch quantities as to hurt them; but they will, if they can; and opportunities fometimes offer, efpecially to thofe who are in the boats; for ftrong liquor being an article much in demand, fo that, without it, fcarcely a fingle Slave can be purchafed, it is always at hand.

hand.ʻ And if what is taken from the cafks or bottles, that are for fale, be fupplied with water, they are as full as they were before. The Blacks, who buy the liquor, are the lofers by the adulteration; but often the people, who cheat them, are the greateft fufferers.

The article of Women, likewife, contributes largely to the lofs of our Seamen. When they are on fhore, they often, from their known, thoughtlefs imprudence, involve themfelves, on this account, in quarrels with the Natives, and, if not killed upon the fpot, are frequently poifoned. On fhip-board, they may be re-ftrained, and in fome fhips they are; but fuch reftraint is far from being general. It depends much upon the difpofition, and attention, of the Captain. When I was in the trade, I knew feveral commanders of African fhips, who were prudent, refpectable men, and who maintained a proper difcipline and regularity in their veffels; but there were too many of a different character. In fome fhips, perhaps in the moft, the licenfe allowed, in this parti-cular, was almoft unlimited. Moral turpitude was feldom confidered, but they who took care to do the fhip's bufinefs, might, in other re-fpects, do what they pleafed. Thefe exceffes, if they do not induce fevers, at leaft, render the

C 2   conftitution

conftitution lefs able to fupport them; and lewdnefs, too frequently, terminates in death.

The rifk of infurrections is to be added. Thefe, I believe, are always meditated ; for the Men Slaves are not, eafily, reconciled to their confinement, and treatment ; and if attempted, they are feldom fuppreffed without confiderable lofs ; and fometimes they fucceed, to the deftruction of a whole fhip's company at once. Seldom a year paffes, but we hear of one or more fuch cataftrophes : and we likewife hear, fometimes, of Whites and Blacks involved, in one moment, in one common ruin, by the gunpowder taking fire, and blowing up the fhip.

How far the feveral caufes, I have enumerated, 'may refpectively operate, I cannot fay : the fact however is fure, that a great number of our Seamen perifh in the Slave Trade. Few fhips, comparatively, are either blown up, or totally cut off, but fome are. Of the reft, I have known fome that have loft half their people, and fome a larger proportion. I am far from faying, that it is always, or even often, thus; but, I believe, I fhall ftate the matter fufficiently low, if I fuppofe, that, at leaft, one fifth part of thofe who go from England to the Coaft of Africa, in fhips which

trade

trade for Slaves, never return from thence. I dare not depend, too much, upon my memory, as to the number of ships, and men, employed in the Slave Trade more than thirty years ago ; nor do I know what has been the ftate of the trade fince ; therefore I fhall not attempt to make calculations. But, as I cannot but form fome opinion upon the fubject, I judge it probable, that the collective fum of Seamen, who go, from all our ports, to Africa, within the courfe of a year, (taking Guinea in the extenfive fenfe, from Goree or Gambia, and including the coaft of Angola,) cannot be lefs than eight thoufand ; and if, upon an average of fhips and feafons, a fifth part of thefe die, the annual lofs is fifteen hundred. I believe thofe, who have taken pains to make more exact enquiries, will deem my fuppofition to be very moderate.

Thus much concerning the firft evil, the Lofs of Seamen and Subjects, which the nation fuftains, by the African Slave Trade.

2. There is a fecond, which either is, or ought to be, deemed of importance, confidered in a political light. I mean, the dreadful effects of this trade, upon the minds of thofe who are engaged in it. There are, doubtlefs, exceptions, and I would, willingly, except myfelf.

myſelf. But, in general, I know of no method of getting money, not even that of robbery, for it, upon the highway, which has a
more direct tendency to efface the moral ſenſe,
to rob the heart of every gentle and humane
diſpoſition, and to harden it, like ſteel, againſt
all impreſſions of ſenſibility.

Uſually, about two-thirds of a cargo of
Slaves are males. When a hundred and fifty
or two hundred ſtout men, torn from their
native land, many of whom never ſaw the ſea,
much leſs a ſhip, till a ſhort ſpace before they
are embarked; who have, probably, the ſame
natural prejudice againſt a white man, as we
have againſt a black; and who often bring with
them an apprehenſion that they are bought to
be eaten : I ſay, when thus circumſtanced, it
is not to be expected that they will, tamely,
reſign themſelves to their ſituation. It is always taken for granted, that they will attempt
to gain their liberty, if poſſible. Accordingly,
as we dare not truſt them, we receive them on
board, from the firſt, as enemies : and before
their number exceeds, perhaps, ten or fifteen,
they are all put in irons; in moſt ſhips, two
and two together. And frequently, they are
not thus confined, as they might, moſt conve-
niently, ſtand or move, the right hand and
foot of one to the left of the other ; but acroſs,
that

that is, the hand and foot of each on the same side, whether right or left, are fettered together: so that they cannot move, either hand or foot, but with great caution, and with perfect consent. Thus they must sit, walk and lie, for many months, (sometimes for nine or ten,) without any mitigation or relief, unless they are sick.

In the night they are confined below, in the day-time (if the weather be fine) they are upon deck; and as they are brought up, by pairs, a chain is put through a ring upon their irons, and this is likewise locked down to the ring-bolts, which are fastened at certain intervals upon the deck. These, and other precautions, are no more than necessary; especially, as while the number of Slaves increases, that of the people, who are to guard them, is diminished, by sickness, or death, or by being absent in the boats: so that, sometimes, not ten men can be mustered, to watch, night and day, over two hundred, besides having all the other business of the ship to attend.

That these precautions are so often effectual, is much more to be wondered at, than that they sometimes fail. One unguarded hour, or minute, is sufficient to give the Slaves the
oppor-

opportunity they are always waiting for. An attempt to rife upon the fhip's company, brings on inftantaneous and horrid war; for, when they are once in motion, they are defperate; and where they do not conquer, they are feldom quelled without much mifchief and bloodfhed, on both fides.

Sometimes, when the Slaves are ripe for an infurrection, one of them will impeach the affair; and then neceffity, and the ftate policy, of thefe fmall, but moft abfolute governments, enforce maxims directly contrary to the nature of things. The traitor to the caufe of liberty is careffed, rewarded, and deemed an honeft fellow. The patriots, who formed and animated the plan, if they can be found out, muft be treated as villains, and punifhed, to intimidate the reft. Thefe punifhments, in their nature and degree, depend upon the fovereign will of the Captain. Some are content with inflicting fuch moderate punifhment, as may fuffice for an example. But unlimited power, inftigated by revenge, and where the heart, by a long familiarity with the fufferings of Slaves, is become callous, and infenfible to the pleadings of humanity, is terrible.

I have

I have feen them fentenced to unmerciful whippings, continued till the poor creatures have not had power to groan under their mifery, and hardly a fign of life has remained. I have feen them agonizing for hours, I believe, for days together, under the torture of the thumb-fcrews; a dreadful engine, which, if the fcrew be turned by an unrelenting hand, can give intolerable anguifh. There have been inftances in which cruelty has proceeded ftill further; but, as I hope they are few, and I can mention but one, from my own knowledge, I fhall but mention it.

I have often heard a Captain, who has been long fince dead, boaft of his conduct in a former voyage, when his Slaves attempted to rife upon him. After he had fuppreffed the infurrection, he fat in judgment upon the infurgents; and not only, in cold blood, adjudged feveral of them, I know not how many, to die, but ftudied, with no fmall attention, how to make death as excruciating to them as poffible. For my reader's fake, I fupprefs the recital of particulars.

Surely, it muft be allowed, that they who are long converfant with fuch fcenes as thefe, are liable to imbibe a fpirit of ferocioufnefs,

and

and favage infenfibility, of which human nature, depraved as it is, is not, ordinarily, capable. If thefe things be true, the reader will
admit the poffibility of a fact, that was in
current report, when I was upon the Coaft, and
the truth of which, though I cannot now au-
thenticate it, I have no reafon to doubt.

A Mate of a fhip, in a long-boat, purchafed
a young woman, with a fine child, of about a
year old, in her arms. In the night, the
child cried much, and difturbed his fleep. He
rofe up in great anger, and fwore, that if the
child did not ceafe making fuch a noife, he
would prefently filence it. The child continued to cry. At length he rofe up a fecond
time, tore the child from the mother, and
threw it into the fea. The child was foon
filenced indeed, but it was not fo eafy to
pacify the woman : fhe was too valuable to be
thrown overboard, and he was obliged to bear
the found of her lamentations, till he could put
her on board his fhip.

I am perfuaded, that every tender mother,
who feafts her eyes and her mind, when fhe
contemplates the infant in her arms, will com-
miferate the poor Africans.—But why do I
fpeak of one child, when we have heard and
read

read a melancholy ftory, too notorioufly true to admit of contradiction, of more than a hundred grown flaves, thrown into the fea, at one time, from on board a fhip, when frefh water was fcarce; to fix the lofs upon the Underwriters, which otherwife, had they died on board, muft have fallen upon the Owners of the veffel. Thefe inftances are fpecimens of the fpirit produced, by the African Trade, in men, who, once, were no more deftitute of the milk of human kindnefs than our-felves.

Hitherto, I have confidered the condition of the Men Slaves only. From the Women, there is no danger of infurrection, and they are carefully kept from the men; I mean, from the Black men. But——In what I have to offer, on this head, I am far from including every fhip. I fpeak not of what is univerfally, but of what is too commonly, and, I am afraid, too generally, prevalent.

I have already obferved, that the Captain of an African fhip, while upon the Coaft, is abfo-lute in his command; and if he be humane, vigilant, and determined, he has it in his power to protect the miferable; for fcarcely any thing can be done, on board the fhip,

without

without his permiffion, or connivance. But
this power is, too feldom, exerted in favour of
the poor Women Slaves.

When we hear of a town taken by ftorm,
and given up to the ravages of an enraged and
licentious army, of wild and unprincipled
Coffacks, perhaps no part of the diftrefs affects
a feeling mind more, than the treatment to
which the women are expofed. But the
enormities frequently committed, in an African
fhip, though equally flagrant, are little known
here, and are confidered, *there*, only as matters
of courfe. When the Women and Girls are
taken on board a fhip, naked, trembling, ter-
rified, perhaps almoft exhaufted with cold,
fatigue, and hunger, they are often expofed to
the wanton rudenefs of white Savages. The
poor creatures cannot underftand the language
they hear, but the looks and manner of the
fpeakers, are fufficiently intelligible. In imagination, the prey is divided, upon the fpot,
and only referved till opportunity offers,
Where refiftance, or refufal, would be utterly
in vain, even the follicitation of confent is
feldom thought of. But I forbear.—This is
not a fubject for declamation. Facts like
thefe, fo certain, and fo numerous, fpeak for
themfelves. Surely, if the advocates for
the

the Slave Trade attempt to plead for it, before the Wives and Daughters of our happy
land, or before thofe who have Wives or
Daughters of their own, they muft lofe their
caufe.

Perhaps fome hard - hearted pleader may
fuggeft, that fuch treatment would indeed be
cruel, in Europe; but the African Women are
Negroes, Savages, who have no idea of the nicer
fenfations which obtain among civilized people.
I dare contradict them in the ftrongeft terms.
I have lived long, and converfed much,
amongft thefe fuppofed Savages. I have often
flept in their towns, in a houfe filled with
goods for trade, with no perfon in the houfe
but myfelf, and with no other door than a
mat; in that fecurity, which no man in
his fenfes would expect, in this civilized
nation, efpecially in this metropolis, without the precaution of having ftrong doors,
ftrongly locked and bolted. And with regard to the women, in Sherbro, where I
was moft acquainted, I have feen many
inftances of modefty, and even delicacy,
which would not difgrace an Englifh woman.
Yet, fuch is the treatment which I have known
permitted, if not encouraged, in many of our
fhips—they have been abandoned, without
reftraint,

reftraint, to the lawlefs will of the firft comer.

Accuftomed thus to defpife, infult, and in- jure the Slaves on board, it may be expected that the conduct of many of our people to the Natives, with whom they trade, is, as far as circumftances admit, very fimilar; and it is fo. They are confidered as a people to be robbed and fpoiled, with impunity. Every art is employed to deceive, and wrong them. And he who has moft addrefs, in this way, has moft to boaft of.

Not an article, that is capable of diminu- tion or adulteration, is delivered genuine, or entire. The fpirits are lowered by water. Falfe heads are put into the kegs that contain the gun-powder; fo that, though the keg ap- pears large, there is no more powder in it, than in a much fmaller. The linen and cotton cloths are opened, and two or three yards, according to the length of the piece, cut off, not from the end, but out of the middle, where it is not fo readily noticed.

The Natives are cheated, in the number, weight, meafure, or quality, of what they purchafe,

purchafe, in every poffible way. And, by habit and emulation, a marvellous dexterity is acquired in thefe practices. And thus the Natives, in their turn, in proportion to their commerce with the Europeans, and (I am forry to add) particularly with the Englifh, become jealous, infidious and revengeful.

They know with whom they deal, and are accordingly prepared;—though they can truft fome fhips and boats, which have treated them with punctuality, and may be trufted by them. A quarrel, fometimes, furnifhes pretext for detaining, and carrying away, one or more of the Natives, which is retaliated, if practicable, upon the next boat that comes to the place, from the fame port. For fo far their vindictive temper is reftrained by their ideas of juftice, that they will not, often, revenge an injury received from a Liverpool fhip, upon one be_ longing to Briftol or London.

They will, ufually, wait with patience, the arrival of one, which, they fuppofe, by her failing from the fame place, has fome connection with that which ufed them ill; and they are fo quick at diftinguifhing our little local differences of language, and cuftoms in a fhip, that before they have been in a fhip five mi-
                                                                    nutes,

nutes, and often before they come on board, they know, with certainty, whether she be from Briftol, Liverpool, or London.

Retaliation on their parts, furnishes a plea for reprizal on ours. Thus, in one place or another, trade is often fufpended, all intercourfe cut off, and things are in a ftate of war; till neceffity, either on the fhip's part, or on theirs, produces overtures of peace, and dictates the price, which the offending party muft pay for it. But it is a warlike peace. We trade under arms; and they are furnifhed with long knives.

For, with a few exceptions, the Englifh and the Africans, reciprocally, confider each other as confummate villains, who are always watching opportunities to do mifchief. In fhort, we have, I fear too defervedly, a very unfavourable character upon the Coaft. When I have charged a Black with unfairnefs and difhonefty, he has anfwered, if able to clear himfelf, with an air of difdain, "What! do "you think I am a White Man?"

Such is the nature, fuch are the concomitants, of the Slave Trade; and fuch is the fchool in which many thoufands of our Seamen

are

are brought up. Can we then wonder at that impatience of fubordination, and that difpo-fition to mutiny, amongft them, which has been, of late, fo loudly complained of, and fo feverely felt? Will not found policy fuggeft, the neceffity, of fome expedient here? Or can found policy fuggeft any, effectual, expedient, but the total fuppreffion of a Trade, which, like a poifonous root, diffufes its malignity into every branch?

The effects which our trade has upon the Blacks, thofe efpecially who come under our power, may be confidered under three heads, —How they are acquired? The mortality they are fubject to! and, How thofe who furvive are difpofed of?

I confine my remarks on the firft head to the Windward Coaft, and can fpeak moft con-fidently of the trade in Sherbro, where I lived. I own, however, that I queftion, if any part of the Windward Coaft is equal to Sherbro, in point of regularity and government. They have no men of great power or property among them; as I am told there are upon the Gold Coaft, at Whidah and Benin. The Sherbro people live much in the patriarchal way. An old man ufually prefides in each

E   town,

town, whofe authority depends more on his
years, than on his poffeffions : and He, who
is called the King, is not eafily diftinguifhed,
either by ftate or wealth, from the reft. But
the different diftricts, which feem to be, in
many refpects, independent of each other, are
incorporated, and united, by means of an in-
ftitution which pervades them all, and is called
The *Purrow*. The perfons of this order, who
are very numerous, feem, very much, to re-
femble the Druids, who once prefided in our
ifland.

The *Purrow* has both the legiflative and
executive authority, and, under their fanction,
there is a police exercifed, which is by no
means contemptible. Every thing belonging
to the *Purrow* is myfterious and fevere, but,
upon the whole, it has very good effects; and
as any man, whether bond or free, who will
fubmit to be initiated into their myfteries, may
be admitted of the Order, it is a kind of
Common-wealth. And, perhaps, few people
enjoy more, fimple, political freedom, than the
inhabitants of Sherbro, belonging to the *Pur-*
row, (who are not flaves,) further than they
are bound by their own inftitutions. Private
property is tolerably well fecured, and violence
is much fuppreffed.

The

The ftate of Slavery, among thefe wild bar-
barous people, as we efteem them, is much
milder than in our colonies. For as, on the
one hand, they have no land in high cultiva-
tion, like our Weft-India plantations, and
thcrefore no call for that exceffive, uninter-
mitted labour, which exhaufts our Slaves; fo,
on the other hand, no man is permitted to
draw blood, even from a Slave. If he does,
he is liable to a ftrict inquifition; for the
Purrow laws will not allow a private indivi-
dual to fhed blood. A man may fell his flave,
if he pleafes; but he may not wantonly abufe
him. The laws likewife punifh fome fpecies
of theft, with flavery; and in cafes of adultery, which are very common, as polygamy is
the cuftom of the country, both the woman,
and the man who offends with her, are liable
to be fold for Slaves, unlefs they can fatisfy
the hufband, or unlefs they are redeemed by
their friends.

Among thefe unenlightened Blacks, it is a
general maxim, that if a man fteals, or breaks
a moveable, as a mufket, for inftance, the offence may be nearly compenfated, by putting
another mufket in its place; but offences,
which cannot be repaired in kind, as adultery,
admit of no fatisfaction, till the injured perfon

declares

declares, that He is fatisfied. So that, if a
rich man feduces the wife of a poor man, he
has it in his power to change places with him ;
for he may fend for every article in his houfe,
one by one, till he fays, " I have enough."
The only alternative, is perfonal flavery.

I fuppofe, bribery and influence may have
their effects in Guinea, as they have in fome
other countries; but their laws, in the main,
are wife and good, and, upon the whole, they
have confiderable operation ; and therefore, I
believe, many of the Slaves purchafed in
Sherbro, and probably upon the whole Windward Coaft, are convicts, who have forfeited
their liberty, by breaking the laws of their
country.

But, I apprehend, that the neighbourhood
of our fhips, and the defire of our goods, are
motives, which often pufh the rigour of the
laws to an extreme, which would not be ex-
acted, if they were left to themfelves.

But Slaves are the ftaple article of the traffic ;
and though a confiderable number may have
been born near the fea, I believe the bulk of
them are brought from far. I have reafon to
think, that fome travel more than a thoufand
miles,

miles, before they reach the fea-coaft. Whether there may be convicts amongft thefe likewife, or what proportion they may bear to thofe who are taken prifoners in war, it is impoffible to know.

I judge, the principal fource of the Slave Trade, is, the wars which prevail among the Natives. Sometimes, thefe wars break out between thofe who live near the fea. The Englifh, and other Europeans, have been charged with fomenting them; I believe (fo far as concerns the Windward Coaft) unjuftly. That fome would do it, if they could, I doubt not; but I do not think they can have opportunity. Nor is it needful they fhould interfere. Thoufands, in our own country, wifh for war, becaufe they fatten upon its fpoils.

Human nature is much the fame in every place, and few people will be willing to allow, that the *Negroes* in Africa are better than themfelves. Suppofing, therefore, they wifh for European goods, may not they wifh to purchafe them from a fhip juft arrived? Of courfe, they muft wiih for Slaves to go to market with; and if they have not Slaves, and think themfelves ftrong enough to invade

their

their neighbours, they will probably wish for war.—And if once they wish for it, how easy is it to find, or make, pretexts for breaking an inconvenient peace; or (after the example of greater heroes, of Christian name) to make depredations, without condescending to assign any reasons.

I verily believe, that the far greater part of the wars, in Africa, would cease; if the Europeans would cease to tempt them, by offering goods for Slaves. And though they do not bring legions into the field, their wars are bloody. I believe, the captives reserved for sale, are fewer than the slain.

I have not sufficient data to warrant calculation, but, I suppose, not less than one hundred thousand Slaves are exported, annually, from all parts of Africa, and that more than one half, of these, are exported in English bottoms.

If but an equal number are killed in war, and if many of these wars are kindled by the incentive of selling their prisoners; what an annual accumulation of blood must there be, crying against the nations of Europe concerned in this trade, and particularly against our own!

I have,

I have, often, been gravely told, as a proof that the Africans, however hardly treated, deferve but little compaffion, that they are a people fo deftitute of natural affection, that it is common, among them, for parents to fell their children, and children their parents. And, I think, a charge, of this kind, is brought againft them, by the refpectable author of *Spectacle de la Nature*. But he muft have been mifinformed. I never heard of one inftance of either, while I ufed the Coaft.

One article more, upon this head, is Kidnapping, or ftealing free people. Some people fuppofe, that the Ship Trade is rather the ftealing, than the buying of Slaves. But there is enough to lay to the charge of the fhips, without accufing them falfely. The flaves, in general, are bought, and paid for. Sometimes, when goods are lent, or trufted on fhore, the trader voluntarily leaves a free perfon, perhaps his own fon, as a hoftage, or pawn, for the payment; and, in cafe of default, the hoftage is carried off, and fold; which, however hard upon him, being in confequence of a free ftipulation, cannot be deemed unfair. There have been inftances of unprincipled Captains, who, at the clofe of what they fuppofed their laft voyage, and when

when

when they had no intention of revifiting the Coaft, have detained, and carried away, free people with them; and left the next fhip, that fhould come from the fame port, to rifk the confequences. But thefe actions, I hope, and believe, are not common.

With regard to the Natives, to fteal a free man or woman, and to fell them on board a fhip, would, I think, be a more difficult, and more dangerous attempt, in Sherbro, than in London. But I have no doubt, that the traders who come, from the interior parts of Africa, at a great diftance, find opportunity, in the courfe of their journey, to pick up. ftragglers, whom they may meet in their way: This branch of oppreffion, and robbery, would likewife fail, if the temptation to it were removed.

I have, to the beft of my knowledge, pointed out the principal fources, of that immenfe fupply of Slaves, which furnifhes fo large an exportation every year. If all that are taken on board the fhips, were to furvive the voyage, and be landed in good order, poffibly the Englifh, French, and Dutch iflands, and colonies, would be foon overftocked, and fewer fhips would fail to the Coaft. But a
larger

large abatement muft be made for mortality. —After what I have already faid of their treatment, I fhall now, that I am again to confider them on board the fhips, confine myfelf to this point.

In the Portuguefe fhips, which trade from Brafil to the Gold Coaft and Angola, I believe a heavy mortality is not frequent. The Slaves have room, they are not put in irons, (I fpeak from information only,) and are humanely treated.

With our fhips, the great objeft is, to be full. When the fhip is there, it is thought defirable, fhe fhould take as many as poffible. The cargo of a veffel of a hundred tons, or little more, is calculated to purchafe from two hundred and twenty to two hundred and fifty Slaves. Their lodging-rooms below the deck, which are three, (for the men, the boys, and the women,) befides a place for the fick, are fometimes more than five feet high, and fometimes lefs; and this height is divided towards the middle, for the Slaves lie in two rows, one above the other, on each fide of the fhip, clofe to each other, like books upon a fhelf. I have known them fo clofe,

F   that

that the shelf would not, eafily, contain one more.

And I have known a white man fent down among the men, to lay them in thefe rows to the greateft advantage, fo that as little fpace as poffible might be loft. Let it be obferved, that the poor creatures, thus cramped for want of room, are likewife in irons, for the moft part both hands and feet, and two together, which makes it difficult for them to turn or move, to attempt either to rife or to lie down, without hurting themfelves, or each other. Nor is the motion of the fhip, efpecially her heeling, or ftoop on one fide, when under fail, to be admitted; for this, as they lie athwart, or acrofs the fhip, adds to the uncomfortablenefs of their lodging, efpecially to thofe who lie on the leeward, or leaning fide of the veffel.

Dire is the toffing, deep the groans.——

The heat and the fmell of thefe rooms, when the weather will not admit of the Slaves being brought upon deck, and of having their rooms cleaned every day, would be, almoft, infupportable, to a perfon not accuftomed

tomed to them. If the Slaves and their rooms
can be conftantly aired, and they are not detained too long on board, perhaps there are not
many die ; but the contrary is often their
lot. They are kept down, by the weather, to
breathe a hot and corrupted air, fometimes
for a week : this, added to the galling of their
irons, and the defpondency which feizes their
fpirits, when thus confined, foon becomes
fatal. And every morning, perhaps, more
inftances than one are found, of the living
and the dead, like the Captives of Mezentius,
faftened together.

Epidemical fevers and fluxes, which fill
the fhip with noifome and noxious effluvia,
often break out, infect the Seamen likewife,
and the Oppreffors, and the Oppreffed, fall by
the fame ftroke. I believe, nearly one half of
the Slaves on board, have, fometimes, died;
and that the lofs of a third part, in thefe circumftances, is not unufual. The fhip, in
which I was Mate, left the Coaft with Two
Hundred and Eighteen Slaves on board; and
though we were not much affected by epidemical diforders, I find, by my journal of that
voyage, (now before me,) that we buried
Sixty-two on our paffage to South-Carolina,
exclufive

exclufive of thofe which died before we left the Coaft, of which I have no account.

I believe, upon an average between the more healthy, and the more fickly voyages, and including all contingencies, One Fourth of the whole purchafe may be allotted to the article of Mortality. That is, if the Englifh fhips purchafe *Sixty Thoufand* Slaves annually, upon the whole extent of the Coaft, the annual lofs of lives cannot be much lefs than *Fifteen Thoufand.*

I am now to fpeak of the furvivors.—When the fhips make the land, (ufually the Weft-India iflands,) and have their port in view after having been four, five, fix weeks, or a longer time, at fea, (which depends much upon the time that paffes before they can get into the permanent Trade Winds, which blow from the North-Eaft and Eaft acrofs the Atlantic,) then, and not before, they venture to releafe the Men Slaves from their irons. And then, the fight of the land, and their freedom from long and painful confinement, ufually excite in them a degree of alacrity, and a tranfient feeling of joy——

The prifoner leaps to lofe his chains.

But,

But, this joy is short-lived indeed. The condition of the unhappy Slaves is in a continual progress from bad to worse. Their case is truly pitiable, from the moment they are in a state of slavery, in their own country; but it may be deemed a state of case and liberty, compared with their situation on board our ships.

Yet, perhaps, they would wish to spend the remainder of their days on ship board, could they know, before-hand, the nature of the servitude which awaits them, on shore; and that the dreadful hardships and sufferings they have already endured, would, to the most of them, only terminate in excessive toil, hunger, and the excruciating tortures of the cart-whip, inflicted at the caprice of an unfeeling Overseer, proud of the power allowed him of punishing whom, and when, and how he pleases.

I hope the Slaves, in our islands, are better treated now, than they were, at the time when I was in the trade. And even then, I know, there were Slaves, who, under the care and protection of humane masters, were, comparatively, happy. But I saw and heard
enough

enough to fatisfy me, that their condition, in general, was wretched to the extreme. However, my ftay in Antigua and St. Chriftopher's (the only iflands I vifited) was too fhort, to qualify me for faying much, from my own certain knowledge, upon this painful fubject. Nor is it needful:—Enough has been offered by feveral refpectable writers, who have had opportunity of collecting furer, and fuller information.

One thing I cannot omit, which was told me by the Gentleman to whom my fhip was configned, at Antigua, in the year 1751, and who was, himfelf, a Planter. He faid, that calculations had been made, with all poffible exactnefs, to determine which was the preferable, that is, the moft faving method of managing Slaves:——

" Whether, to appoint them moderate
" work, plenty of provifion, and fuch
" treatment, as might enable them to
" protract their lives to old age ?" Or,

" By rigoroufly ftraining their ftrength to
" the utmoft, with little relaxation,
" hard fare, and hard ufage, to wear
" them out before they became ufelefs,
                                    " and

" and unable to do fervice; and then,
" to buy new ones, to fill up their
" places ?"

He farther faid, that thefe fkilful calcu-
lators had determined in favour of the latter
mode, as much the cheaper; and that he
could mention feveral eftates, in the ifland of
Antigua, on which, it was feldom known,
that a Slave had lived above nine years.——
Ex pede Herculem!

When the Slaves are landed for fale, (for in
the Leeward Iflands they are ufually fold on
fhore,) it may happen, that after a long fe-
paration in different parts of the fhip, when
they are brought together in one place, fome,
who are nearly related, may recognize each
other. If, upon fuch a meeting, pleafure
fhould be felt, it can be but momentary.
The fale difperfes them wide, to different
parts of the ifland, or to different iflands.
Hufbands and Wives, Parents and Children,
Brothers and Sifters, muft fuddenly part again,
probably to meet no more.

After a careful perufal of what I have
written, weighing every paragraph diftinctly,
I can

I can find nothing to retract. As it is not easy to write altogether with coolness, upon this business, and especially not easy to me, who have formerly been so deeply engaged in it; I have been jealous, left the warmth of imagination might have insensibly seduced me, to aggravate and overcharge some of the horrid features, which I have attempted to delineate, of the African Trade. But, upon a strict review, I am satisfied.

I have apprized the reader, that I write from memory, after an interval of more than thirty years. But at the same time, I believe, many things which I saw, heard and felt, upon the Coast of Africa, are so deeply engraven in my memory, that I can hardly forget, or greatly mistake them, while I am capable of remembering any thing. I am certainly not guilty of wilful misrepresentation. And, upon the whole, I dare appeal to the Great Searcher of hearts, in whose presence I write, and before whom I, and my readers, must all shortly appear, that (with the restrictions and exceptions I have made) I have advanced nothing, but what, to the best of my judgment and conscience, is true.

I have

I have likewife written without folicitation, and fimply from the motive I have already affigned; a conviction, that the fhare I have for merly had in the trade, binds me, in confcience, to throw what light I am able upon the fubject, now it is likely to become a point of Parliamentary inveftigation.

No one can have lefs intereft in it, than I have at prefent, further than as I am interefted by the feelings of humanity, and a regard for the honour, and welfare of my country.

Though unwilling to give offence to a fingle perfon; in fuch a caufe, I ought not to be afraid of offending many, by declaring the truth; if, indeed, there can be many, whom even intereft can prevail upon to contradict the common fenfe of mankind, by pleading for a commerce, fo iniquitous, fo cruel, fo oppreffive, fo deftructive, as the African Slave Trade!

6

F I N I S,

1. MESSIAH. Fifty Difcourfes on the Series of Scriptural Paffages, which form the Subject of the celebrated ORATORIO OF HANDEL. Preached in the Years 1784 and 1785, in the Parifh Church of St. Mary Woolnoth, Lombard-Street. 2 Vols. 8vo. Price 12 s. bound.

2. A SERMON on the Death of the late DR. CONYERS. Price 6 d.

3. Apologia: four Letters to a Minifter of an independant Church, by a Minifter of the Church of England. Price 2 s.

4. Letters and Sermons, with a Review of Ecclefiaftical Hiftory, and Hymns. 6 Vols. 12mo. Price 15 s. fewed, 18 s. in plain binding, or 21 s. bound in calf and lettered.

CONTAINING

* 1. An Authentic Narrative of fome interefting Particulars in the Life of ●*** ******. 2 s.

* 2. OLNEY Hymns. 2 s.

* 3. OMICRON's Letters, complete. 2 s. 6 d.

* 4. CARDIPHONIA, or the Utterance of the Heart. 2 Vols. 7 s.

5. Twenty-feven Sermons.

6. A Review of Ecclefiaftical Hiftory.

☞ Such Articles as are marked * may be had alone at the prices affixed.

Printed for J. BUCKLAND in Pater-nofter Row; and J. JOHNSON, Nº 72, St. Paul' Church-Yard.

www.ingramcontent.com/pod-product-compliance
Lightning Source LLC
Chambersburg PA
CBHW022205020726
47496CB00008B/2893